HAL•LEONARD

INSTRUMENTAL
PLAY-ALONG

AUDIO
ACCESS
INCLUDED

PLAYBACK+
peed • Pitch • Balance • Loop

TROMBONE

A NEW MUSICAL
WICKED

To access audio visit:
www.halleonard.com/mylibrary
Enter Code
8677-8833-5676-2456

ISBN: 978-1-4234-4972-0

HAL•LEONARD®

7777 W. BLUEMOUND RD. P.O. BOX 13819 MILWAUKEE, WI 53213

Visit Hal Leonard Online at
www.halleonard.com

AS LONG AS YOU'RE MINE

Music and Lyrics by
STEPHEN SCHWARTZ

TROMBONE

DANCING THROUGH LIFE

TROMBONE

Words and Music by
STEPHEN SCHWARTZ

DEFYING GRAVITY

TROMBONE

Words and Music by
STEPHEN SCHWARTZ

Allegro, as before

FOR GOOD

TROMBONE

Words and Music by
STEPHEN SCHWARTZ

I COULDN'T BE HAPPIER

TROMBONE

Words and Music by
STEPHEN SCHWARTZ

I'M NOT THAT GIRL

TROMBONE

Words and Music by
STEPHEN SCHWARTZ

NO GOOD DEED

TROMBONE

Words and Music by
STEPHEN SCHWARTZ

ONE SHORT DAY

TROMBONE

Music and Lyrics by
STEPHEN SCHWARTZ

POPULAR

TROMBONE

Words and Music by
STEPHEN SCHWARTZ

WHAT IS THIS FEELING?

Words and Music by
STEPHEN SCHWARTZ

TROMBONE

THE WIZARD AND I

TROMBONE

Words and Music by
STEPHEN SCHWARTZ

WONDERFUL

TROMBONE

Music and Lyrics by
STEPHEN SCHWARTZ

NO ONE MOURNS THE WICKED

TROMBONE

Words and Music by
STEPHEN SCHWARTZ

Flowing, not too slow